ONE SHOE MARCHING TOWARDS HEAVEN

ONE SHOE MARCHING TOWARDS HEAVEN

Poems

≈≈≈≈≈≈≈≈≈≈≈≈≈≈≈≈≈≈≈≈≈≈≈≈≈≈≈≈≈≈≈≈≈≈≈

Bro. Yao (Hoke S. Glover III)

AFRICA WORLD PRESS
Trenton | London | Cape Town | Nairobi | Addis Ababa | Asmara | Ibadan | New Delhi

AFRICA WORLD PRESS
541 West Ingham Avenue | Suite B
Trenton, New Jersey 08638

Copyright © 2020 Bro. Yao (Hoke S. Glover III)

All rights reserved. No part of this publication may be reproduced, stored in a retrieval system or transmitted in any form or by any means electronic, mechanical, photocopying, recording or otherwise without the prior written permission of the publisher.

Cover picture credit: Oleg Magni
Cover design: Ashraful Haque
Book design: Lemlem Tadesse

Cataloging-in-Publication Data may be obtained from the Library of Congress.

ISBNs: 978-1-56902-690-8 (HB)
      978-1-56902-691-5 (PB)

Previously Published Poems

"Koan #23," "Koan #3," and "The Miner Speaks of the Underground" published in the *Langston Hughes Review*.
"Putting Niggers to Rest" and "Winter's Blues" published in *Rattle Magazine*.
"Jimmy Ballard," "Speaker," and "Mountain" published in African-American Review.
"A Son Confesses" and "Riff on Patriotism and Nostalgia" published in *JoINT Literary Magazine*.

Contents

Notes on the Poems xi
Brief Introduction and Acknowledgements 1
Bro. Yao Is a Poem 3
beginning 7
    koan #1: there's always a way out 9
    hell poem #2 10
    speaker 11
    thief said 13
    koan #23: falling away 14
    truth commission (south africa 1995) 15
    koan #34 16
    putting the niggers to rest 17
begin again 21
    koan #128 23
    koan #18: working on what's spoiled 24
    broken glass 25
    train 27
    Love Song 29

My Father Rides his Horses into the Distance 30

Jimmy Ballard 32

Riff on Patriotism and Nostalgia 33

The Angel Speaks of Being Born Black 36

Winter's Blues 38

A Son Confesses 39

Burned Down 41

koan #68: a final blue 42

return 43

holy men I 45

koan #11: no way 47

Double Consciousness 48

good enuff 49

koan #3: difficulty at the beginning 51

untitled 52

heaven 55

koan #10: across the ice 57

Mountain 59

Heaven #1 60

What Door Opens Like This 62

Heaven #2 63

for karla 65

onward 67

code: the koans begin 69

Revisiting the Underground 70

koan #7: the nationalist speaks of war 74

CONTENTS

Song for The Country 75
Solo on Rage 76
when massa speak of freedom 78
my dream starring the devil 79
Elijah Muhammad 82
everafter 85
koan # 57: the blowing wind 87
Home 88
the gods 90
on reading Jack Gilbert too late at night 92
free black space 93
koan #58: late joy 95
for baraka 96
koan #64: not yet forever 97
The Miner Speaks of the Underground 98

Notes on the Poems

Koans are paradoxes and riddles used in the Zen tradition to help practitioners unravel the nature of thought.

The I-Ching is an ancient Chinese book of wisdom that presents 64 lined structures called hexagrams made up of lines that represent yin and yang. Together the hexagrams are said to represent the fundamental changes all of reality alternates through.

Koans presented here correspond to I-Ching hexagrams. Interested readers may refer to those hexagrams to deepen their understanding of the text.

Though there are only 64 hexagrams in the I-Ching, the author is constructing a larger manuscript of koans that will contain 128. In some cases the numbers presented here reflect the work of that manuscript and are higher than 64.

Brief Introduction and Acknowledgements

My first book *Inheritance* (Willow, 2017) compiled poems from the first three decades of my poetic life and was centered around the theme of family. *One Shoe Marching Towards Heaven* reflects the same poetic journey from a different vantage. This manuscript works to piece together my diverse interests in Chinese culture, jazz, and the pursuit of a simple voice that captures African-American wisdom.

The title, *One Shoe Marching Towards Heaven,* is a koan. Koans function as teaching tools in the Zen tradition for monks working towards enlightenment. The Koans presented here strive to capture the simple voice of African-American wisdom speakers in a form that defies the boundaries of our literature. The numerical arc of the koans corresponds to the I-Ching. This book connects African-American culture with Asian culture. Though China is not referenced in the book, Chinese culture and wisdom functions as third rail of cultural infrastructure that informs much of the work.

This is a book that is somehow about heaven. Heaven within the I-Ching is the place above, and location of the Creative. Earth is the place of the receptive. Heaven and Earth work together towards balance. Heaven is not a destination in the afterworld. It is an active force in everyday life working with the forces of earth towards balance. It is humans in between earth that play out the will and work of the cosmos.

I would like to thank first and foremost Afaa M. Weaver whose work connects the beauty of Chinese wisdom and culture with the beauty of African-American wisdom and culture. Without Afaa, I would not imagine a work like this making it into the world.

Second I would like to thank Terence Nicholson whose work as visual artist, hip-hop musician, and martial artist constantly expands my vision of human potential.

I would also like to thank Kassahun Checole for agreeing to publish this work. His work as an African/African-American publisher for decades is one of the greatest contributions to African diasporic literature in our time.

I would also like to thank Karla Wilkerson Glover for reading my poems, often in the middle of the night and supporting my poetic career over the decades.

Special thanks to Jon Miller, Laura Neal, Brian Gilmore, Abdul Ali, Dr. Valerie Prince, Randall Horton, Sarah Trembath, Asha French, Samuel Miranda, Karla Wilkerson-Glover, and Dr. Monifa Love for reading and commenting on the editing of the manuscript. I am eternally grateful.

I would also like to thank all of those people in my poetic community who have supported my work and journey over the years.

Bro. Yao Is a Poem

> "We want freedom, prophecies of ancient wisdom…"
> —dead prez, "We Want Freedom"

The myth goes that the Buddhist monk Bodhidharma walked from what is now India to China to teach meditation practices to Shaolin monks. When Bodhidharma arrived at Shaolin, he grew dismayed to find that the monks were so flabby and out of shape that they would fall asleep whenever they began to meditate. To bring the monks to physical fitness so they could properly learn meditation, Bodhidharma studied the fighting styles of animals to develop a series of exercises. This sequence of movement evolved into the collection of fighting techniques commonly known as kung-fu.

*

Here's something that is not a myth: If you're with Bro. Yao in a moment of stillness, say a meeting or an extended lull in the conversation, look over at him and you might see him engaged in slow motions, the practice of tai chi forms. His doodles are hexagrams, or divinations from the *I-Ching*. For Yao, there is no separation between tai chi and life. There is no separation between ancient wisdom and life. This is a hard fought discipline. A radical change of perspective from the way most of us are taught to see. This is also the essence of the *Tao Te Ching*, that book of Chinese scriptures that often emphasizes seeing the unity in all things. The *Tao* informs us that the wise person, "[h]olding all things within himself he preserves the Great Unity which cannot be ruled or divided."

*

Though I knew that the myth of Bodhidharma's invention of the martial arts is just that, a myth, a fiction designed to explain the origins of something with irretrievably lost origins, I was desperate so I purchased a boxing dummy. At the time I slept poorly, and like the Shaolin monks of legend, I was flabby and out of shape, and when I tried to conjure the meditative trance required to write fiction, I'd often drift off to sleep. I was operating under the theory (now proven false) that if I felt the pangs of drowsiness during a writing session, I'd simply hop up, strap on boxing gloves and spar a few rounds after which I'd return to the blank page invigorated and ready to slip into the dream needed to write. But what if there is no dream? What if wakefulness and dreaming, at least when it comes to the act of creation, is one and the same? In that case *writing* doesn't begin and end when one is sitting before a blank page. In that case one is always writing, as one's heart is always in motion. Here we see how Bro. Yao is able to achieve the scripture-like effects of his poetry. The poem is not a thing that is separate from him. That is an illusion. Bro. Yao himself is the poem.

This discipline is most readily observed in the ruminative koans spread throughout the book. In Yao's poetry I've always seen the influence of Robert Hayden and Stanley Plumly, poets who used sharp observation and precision to elucidate the humanity of the often difficult people who raised them—that element remains, for sure, but in this work Yao merges that with the patience and urgency of ancient wisdoms, not just in the koans, but particularly in the koans. These poems don't so much as approximate the voice of Zen koans, as the form here is made anew, to examine the paradoxes and contradictions of modern black life.

In "Koan #1.1-There's Always a Way Out-the Creative" Yao writes "you could become/ more perfect slave/ a more perfect union/ free yourself from/ the idea of freedom" and in a few simple lines he challenges the foundational assumptions of America and the ideas we accept and even hold dear, but rarely interrogate. It is provocative, for sure, and almost maddening. Jonathan Star, translator of *Tao Te Ching: The Definitive Edition* writes in his introduction that the verses of the *Tao* are often "impenetrable by design...they are not meant to be grasped by the rational mind alone; their inner meanings were meant to be discovered through one's own insight and spiritual penetration." Though I wouldn't describe Bro. Yao's poetry as impenetrable, like the *Tao*, it does call on one to bring their entire self—both the yin and the yang—to bear.

Opening the self to these poems is a doorway perhaps to that state of contentment Yao calls free black space. As he writes in the poem of the same name: "...the sea is in me. the sea is in us."

Rion Scott Annapolis, Md.

May 16th, 2020

beginning

koan #1: there's always a way out

even in the beginning
in the first book of nigger
you could escape

by submission
you could become
more perfect slave
more perfect union

free yourself from
the idea of freedom

hell poem #2

how will the angels
and gods appear
among the wretched?

will they shine?

        gleaming albatross
        of heat and light

or will they be confused
with the flames?

will they conceal themselves
looking like us

whispering
what all
must hear?

speaker

the microphone, the holy object,
the way brothers held it, held the day
get down, get down, do-wop
pips, everybody on the same step,
tommie smith with his fist raised
in the air, the fastest man in the world
wearing gold sneakers, talking nonsense-he
hero of the children who want to run fast
out of the corner store-that shit don't
happen no more, you gotta point out
your candy behind the plexiglass
broken english of capitalism, ghetto
a stairway made out of fried chicken
bones, cigarettes, a mosaic of liquor bottles,
you got to take off the plexi-glass blur
if you want to see, you got to turn
off your radio if you want to hear the speaker
125th back woods stomp in the forest.
i remember the first time we heard the low-end
theory, philosophy of bass, in a car with
the heat on, must've been december, blowing
fog into our hands-we knew it was the move,
craig mack, flava in your ear, nonsense-
"what is he talk'n bout," but it made that other sense
sense that ooze warm through the speaker
our last year in high school where every party
was eric b and rakim, telling me, "you, you
you got it-paid in full", speaker pulse down
in the night on V street behind the tinted windows
where they race the bikes and cars, you can smell
burnt tires in the air, that's it, right there
at the traffic light, red stop sign, you can feel

ONE SHOE MARCHING TOWARDS HEAVEN

the nigger look in your rearview mirror
watch your back, watchout-bass massaging your
ear drums, old school brothers with congos
down in malcolm x park ain't got no electricity
or malcolm's own voice wandering in america's
purgatory on the spools of brown magnetic tape
traveling the sisyphean circle of a cd speaker-
you, you, you got it-soul, not just the sound system
but the system of sound/ break it down, to the old man
outside the subway station who talks out of his head
whose head is
> *mumble dingy tired country all this*
> *nonsense, the president, christmas, pagan*
> *worshippers of the anti-christ of the freakadic*
> *ism of transistors and cds and dvds jesus*
> *was a speaker i is a speaker-what this is now*
> *running through me-i be-i believe*

thief said

it is easier to blame yourself, than require justice.
i gamble on this. justify the steel frame by the
metal mined from the earth. i worship heaven
as the place where they will forget what happened.
i am no more evil than them, for what difference
does it make-if you do not believe?

koan #23: falling away

lord, forgive me
i done stole something
from myself
used it to pay
the man

who stole from me

truth commission (south africa 1995)

zinsili is in the mountains

searching for the truth

in the truth commission

when he closes his eyes

he sees a pendulum with bloody

bodies kabobbed on it

the sound it makes

the time it keeps

has more screams than he can count

koan #34

johnny wrote
a book for slaves
to help them get free

but there's laws
against slaves reading
most slaves can't read.

how many books did Johnny sell?

putting the niggers to rest

all the men who called my father nigger
stand with all the men who have called me nigger
in a line outside the capitol. some just arrive.
they fall into the back of the line saying nigger
nigger, nigger, out into the night light morse code.

there is dust in their mouth mixed with the water
of wisdom, a truth they know that is not nigger
but mixed to mud that is a dirty knowing a broken
record of speech and thought and urge.

there is another line, next to theirs, for the ones
who call me nigger in secret, under their breath
and with their eyes, whispering it between one another
a code, yes, him, they nod, the nigger over there
the niggers over there. look at them.

and all over the world niggers are dying, like speech
whose reality never was, niggers tumbling over niggers
trying to get on top. niggers fighting for the right to
be niggers in the real live world. to cross from fantasy
into the world of flesh, to grab the last boat to America

and there's another line of people who think nigger
and then think, my father, my mother said that, my
grandmother and grandfather said that, nigger
tradition, i do not want to say that, i do not want
to say such a terrible thing, though i am perplexed
by some of them calling themselves that, confused,
why? that's not right, but its still not right to call
them it in secret, under our breath, so terrible.

it is a great conflict, like storms over barren planets

ONE SHOE MARCHING TOWARDS HEAVEN

with no water. that i know nigger is wrong but some
part of nigger still makes sense. to know that feeling
to understand that argument, between warring selves
imagine it a great struggle between reason and passion.

there is a graveyard full of niggers that only the nigger
sayers know of. i've seen the niggers. do you know
any niggers?

and the people who sometimes get called niggers wander
about in camouflage and espionage. they won't stand in line
cuz ain't no niggers allowed in the line, they meander about,
wander with their hands in their pocket singing negro spirituals
so nobody think they listening, so nobody wonder as they
wander, you could say they try to look like niggers knowing
the difference between them and niggers, wearing nigger
like a hoody when necessary, when it's cold outside and
they need something to cover them, to keep the cold out.

they study the speech of the nigger sayers and mix it
gumbo into the speech they speak, and adapt, put a
bass line under it, and make it sound so funky, even hate
seem harmless, like a blade dulled from overuse, like a tool
beaten against the earth so much it grows dull and only
looks like a tool in the hands of the slave on a hot day
with someone screaming over your shoulder WORK!

and the longest line, the one that stretches out
the door, out of the capital city, zigzagging through
richmond and the good south, through day long
drive texas, back up to the northeast, the great lakes
and west through those beautiful states with trees
and land that makes the jaw drop like the canyons,

and the plains, and the deserts, tundra, palm trees
is the line where people think niggers, nigger shit,
jacked up shit, and there is no one who fits
the description to be found. nobody nobody
to be conjured as nigger anywhere around.

begin again

koan #128

show me
you love me
prove
you have the blues

koan #18: working on what's spoiled

if your mother hurts you
be gentle with the memory
gently untangle the knots
as though her hair was like a white woman's
long and stringy, unravel it, and then
braid it again, softly into the night

if your father hurts you, try not
to descend into the fog
of that nigger ain't shit,
many do not know their fathers
or what forest he runs through

still, to this day

work on what has been spoiled
by the heavy rain and storms,
what has lost its luster, the dirt,
the worn shoe shines again
with elbow grease and sweat
know what you must do,
how it done

broken glass

hope is billie's voice raised
to the tone of perfection
so that you know she floated

just out of the range of the melody
to say-things be that way sometime

almost all the time if you come
from where I'm from

sometimes you dream money
and wake up with pennies

other times you dream peace
and wake up at war

black birds in the trash
on sunday, organs medicate
morning for preaching

bad boys roll over
liquor breath in their beds
shake their head at last night,
shoving sheets
between their legs

a cold winter morning
has hope frosted on the windows

write your name in it, steam
out of a tiny cup, nothing last

ONE SHOE MARCHING TOWARDS HEAVEN

forever, all disappears

cold will win against heat
until some fool thinks

to sing i love you, i was loved
this, is what you have done to me

heart break is about eternal resurrection

thin spirit, crackheads
wandering in the early morning
or late night what difference
does it make?

billie's voice blowing
its changing geometry, a flag
shaped by wind and the body
being blown, away

train

down the straight
iron rails
at five

looking out

picking up rocks
hurling them into the woods

heavy
is the weight
in a boy's arm

when he throws the rocks
he throws his whole body

feels the world
in his arm

as the gnats rise
into the air
and graze his eyes

not far from home
he hears the echoes
of his mother's voice

here the train comes
hear the whistle

at five

train

ONE SHOE MARCHING TOWARDS HEAVEN

tracks
gust of wind
the machine makes

a little boy roars in his heart
roars in his heart forever

Love Song

Before I was born and born
to an ambition, my father dreamed
my mother as the woman he would
one day love, not knowing her face
or the innocence she cultivated like
a small cup of tea on a large round
table in the house of my grandparents.

My grandfather's anger rattled the table.
He slammed his hand down, and my mother
sipped calmly from the chipped tea cup.
There was a place near the rim where she
ran her tongue across it. the tiny waves.

I was a dream then, we all are dreams,
nothing is impossible they would tell me.
We are all like the land, boundless and deep.
Stretching into horizons. Beautiful and vast.

When I am singing their song, even now
under the gentle fires of a calm life,
I think of their love, it's shape like clouds
covering a moon at night. Sometimes you
can see through them: the moon there
shining bright, a strange flower in the sky.

My Father Rides his Horses into the Distance

What now she asks
And slams the door
    Violence hidden
    And the sex underneath that
Walk across the room
And cry a little
But don't let nobody see it

    Both of them

Like opposites and ideas
With flesh pasted onto skeletons

    Then the dusk comes
    Then then speeches
    The long rants in heads
    Fights that have no words
    The dead people who could not
    Could not rest, the sun going down,

The old streets of the city
Where once there were horses
    A man singing ice, milk, butter, bread

What it's all about

He goes outside
And talks to the man
In the always winter
    The cold heated by his breath
    He whispers
    And the white smoke rises

He sings the only song he knows
He will not go back into the house

He buys a horse who is too old to run
And grabs the rope and walks him

Down the street and into the night
And the cold swallows him

ONE SHOE MARCHING TOWARDS HEAVEN

Jimmy Ballard

When Jimmy Ballard died
His best friend pulled a stocking cap
Over his head, and confessed to crimes
He had never done, that's how deep
The sadness was

The glory of death is its flash
Men stumble in it, black silk flows
The wind is the ghost of our grip
On the back of the one we've lost
Our head resting on their shoulder

When a man prays on his knees
Either he's righteous or thinks he's not
And that's the only way he can get there
The only thing he can do

I'm lonely for Jimmy to come back
There's a constant tone in the air
Like someone's tuning this life
To another frequency, the season
Has changed the air breathing up my sleeves

Someone solos on his horn forever
He won't take it out of his mouth
And drums rise underneath,
Weapons for the war we cannot see

Riff on Patriotism and Nostalgia

I walk around like, I walk, I walk around
Like I ain't got no country, like I'm dazed

In a strobelit room. In a room where they
Read, where someone is reading from the book,

The book on freedom, big black Bible book,
With pages tissue paper thin, flip 'em too fast

And they tear, thin like toilet paper, thin like
Tissue you use to wipe your nose, thin like

The walls in the house where when somebody,
Somebody gets mad, they punch the wall angry

Clench their fist, and it tears right through.
I heard him whisper next door, I heard 'em

Like secret police, I'm the secret police, the man
Who hears whispers, checks the eyes, I check

The eyes, does he have ghost, does he sing
The national anthem, which national anthem,

Which anthem, which uuhn, which ah-em,
Which dem, which dey, which way does he feel?

Does he sing of freedom and what does he mean,
I mean is it a mean song of freedom, secessionist

Song about splitting the country taken over, the
Country over there, splitting it in half, half

ONE SHOE MARCHING TOWARDS HEAVEN

The folks I know never know what I'm talking
Bout, when I'm talking, they got that patriotism

Tattooed on their shoulder, they got a flexed
Bicep, arm wrestle for ego, put it down, will

Put you down if you talk bout their country,
That's why I walk, walk around like I ain't

Got no country. It's about the color, the red,
The white, and blue, the color of my skin,

Black and blue, which dem, which dey? I got
Three things I am trying to be, one-free, two-

Just like you, and three-me, I mean what
You think the constitution is all about? Shout

Scream your American dream. What have you done?
Now, they pull in the women in bikinis with

Stars and stripes on them, a beer can that means
America, I got it. I got it bad, and that ain't good,

I read the signs, names of cities I ain't supposed
To go to, sides of towns, sundown, bring the ruckus

Sides of town, I'm not. I'm not s'posed to be here,
Amongst all these glimmering lights, I like to eat.

To eat out in my two country, three country,
Country and count all the ways to say

I love you. This fist, this lynch rope, the gold
Medal tied around my neck, this backwards

Running, backwoods dream, this American
Trek towards the sea. What does it do, what

Does it all mean? And I say backstroke, swim
On your back, float, I say walk around, walk,

Walk around like you gotta country, fake it
If you can't make it. Like you gotta do

Do something important, like you been
Studying. Studying the masters.

The Angel Speaks of Being Born Black

After they asked me to come here
My man, they flushed me
Outa heaven and into that sea
Swirling world. Throwing me
Into the river to see if I sink,
Swim or float. Dead weight.
Balloon. Hands treading water.
Under August moon I hear.
I hear the serpent, the river
Singing deep in the earth's gut,
With current, force of wheel
Where it meets the earth. Before
Man learned of its shape its
Spinning, when Fall first
Decided to make the leaves
Dance, make their way gently
To the ground, I was down.
Before man worshipped genius
Which is blessing, birthright
And stone thrown into
The river. It will not float. Spine
Backbone, it's all the same shit. We
Get something and call it will,
Catch spirit but it won't stay
Still. We try to say, talk ourselves
Into being, but we were born
And then born again, way
Up above and way down low,
I can't get no rest, mouth open
While the sky pours rain. Someone
Is singing into the night. No.
No body knows, It's the river,
Water breaking water, angel

Humbled to man, some other
Beauty, some other thing
Who ain't got wings, but still
I sing Power that can't be
Tamed. They'll never know
Never know my name. This
Spinning world. How it hold
Me down. But I'm down with it.

Winter's Blues

Someone waits all day for a letter
And when the mail comes it doesn't

Someone says I love you and the words
Fall like snow towards the warm windows
Of the rich man's house melting in touch
But the touch makes them nothing

Someone loses their name and walks back
Through the woods to find it, but the weather
Has turned the ground white

A Son Confesses

This is whiskey in a man's life
This is my mother's hard work
and apron, a rag, dust.

Here are her feet swollen in shoes.
Here are newspapers on the floor.
Here is yesterday's bruise.

This is my calm courage.
This is my wooden pew.

I go to call my father.
I go to call the moon.

This is the gospel
of wished for never happen.
This is the moon staring one-eye.

See how fire drinks wood.
See how we run.
See how water pools
outside the house.

My father never comes.
My name never rings.

This is how it storms.
This is how it rains.

    See how drunk I am.

        Listen into the dark,

ONE SHOE MARCHING TOWARDS HEAVEN

Hear me howl his name.

It sounds just like mine.

Burned Down

I do not go back to the house
Since it burned down. They told
Me it was beautiful. Such is fire.

The men fought not to save.
It was more sport than anything.
Some of them watched. Water

> *Does not eat flame; flame does*
> *Not eat water. Sometimes day*
> *Is not hot. Water is not always*
>
> *Cold. Fire's absence can still be*
> *Warm. Not all heat is hot, not*
> *All cold cold, unless it's the coldest*

How would I know?

Some people had to throw away
Their clothes, the soot stuffed

Into the fiber. Most days I know
I'll never heal.

> *Ask who am I*
> *To remember what*
> *I was forgetting*

Why? it already happened. To die

In the heat, to dream awake, to run
Into the heat, to dream awake, to run
Towards heaven, to never make it.

koan #68: a final blue

the ship in me has sunk
now I am the sea
the sea in me
deep and blue

return

holy men I

so things have come to this

each body each name
splitting open

each ancestor being born again

sound of the needle
and the tiny whistle

there will be days like this

when all the innocent conversation
will turn to parables

and the dead shall rise
dignified

and that street
you could not stare
in the face

will shed all its sin

behold

ONE SHOE MARCHING TOWARDS HEAVEN

lonely god
in a new skin

speaking through
your mouth

where have you been?

koan #11: no way

when you find your self
among the many selves slaved
you will know the slave

no self,
no slave

no more,
no way

Double Consciousness

Is like schizophrenia
Is like talking to yourself
A trumpet with a mute
Hiding your gun
In the crook of your back
      Like that
So you don't get yourself
Killed, talking shit
Meant for backwoods
And Thanksgiving dinner tables

So when the police come
You don't talk that black
      Side of your brain
Or put your foot down
Or move too quick

Seeing double is double
Consciousness knowing
      Where you stand

Deep in the forest of America
Without a map

      Over there in them trees

      Right dere

      Somewhere

good enuff

not good enuff. not good.
enough. be better. best.
be like the best. be more.
be more careful. come.
come correct. come down
from where you are. come
be   leave. believe. be
something to make
your mama proud. be all.
be all you can be. be it all.
be better. do better. be
best. you was born on
the wrong side of town.
you got it. you gotta work
harder. you gotta try harder.
you gotta breathe deep. you
gotta sleep with one eye
open. you gotta dance
like all eyes on you. you
gotta. i gotcha. i gotcha
in my sight. i gotcha.
i'm watchin ya. this ain't
that hard. ain't that difficult.
find yourself. deep in
that dark night. trace your
shadow. row your boat.
find yourself. there's more.
more to life than trying
to be something. more
than you think? try
wind in may brushing
across your skin. or

ONE SHOE MARCHING TOWARDS HEAVEN

rain. can you count
that high with money
or tasks or what you
imagine to be the things
god wants you to do.
pretty and simple. be.
what you afraid of.
what you think gonna
happen? it may not happen.
maybe it will? maybe
you ain't in the right
place? maybe you sposed
to be doing something
else? maybe your name
was a mistake. maybe
i ain't john. i ain't larry.
maybe i ain't mary or
barbara. maybe it's...
maybe you are the secret
without your clothes
and cell phone. beneath
the eyes that watch
the sun and the moon.
soon you will know.
soon you will come
back to the thing before
your self. soon you will
find out. find an out. get
out.

koan #3: difficulty at the beginning

if you willing
to work
    like a slave
anything
    is possible

untitled

the poet ties shoes
in the morning and thinks
about the knots, the fingertips,
the tiny strings and walking
all day

wind and the car's engine
the shutting of the door,
and the footsteps across
the graveled path pieces
in the orchestra playing
the world behind the world

the apple in the morning
so red she thinks of fire
and wonders at the sun
streaked between the clouds

impossible image

and the taste of salt
which almost burns
and the tough skin
of bread   the teeth
of the hungry   the rest
and belly full

why? is useless
like an ocean
you look at
like a dream
of swimming farther

than you can swim

like a heaven
you run to
like a hill you climb
into the sky
with your feet
still attached to the ground

the poet knows
why some choke
on religion
and is jealous
of that certainty

with wet socks
and dirty underwear
with a spotted shirt
and hunger   memory
and the tiny wounds
from thorns

a burnt smile
and a cross burning
in eternity

with a forest
all around
and no way

heaven

koan #10: across the ice

You walk slowly
Towards tomorrow

With your hair undone
Nappy world

You say beauty
And know it ain't

Easy to come
Easy to see

How everything
Don't really matter

My love
Why did you lie?

When I said heaven
I did not mean gospel

Or conviction or curse
If you wouldn't go

ONE SHOE MARCHING TOWARDS HEAVEN

I did not mean to be mean
To scare and hurt

We are all just animals
That's what they say

Somebody runs behind
Somebody calls out

Somebody sounds
Like a bird, calling

Out into the night
But where is heaven?

Is it freedom?
Would you follow me?

Mountain

When we drive into the black hills
they are black because it is night
and dusk has taken the light left
in this final day of winter and split
the final fight into moans. We see
clouds over head and the trees
pressing into the sky together
like an afro of a mother
whose children have left
the house. Now there is silence
and a rest that breathes through
morning and night, sun and go down.

When we come to not saying,
or saying not what we mean
to say, when we say something
simple and sweet, please
hand me the music of your life,
please dance with me, say you,
say you love me with your body,
or your words. I'll take anything.
I'll scream with magic. I'll go
to the grocery store and pick up
a small bar of chocolate. I'll sit
in the dark under the T.V.'s glowing
light with your leg lapped over mine
and say nothing just feeling the heat.

Heaven #1

Later that day
When I thought
About heaven again,

I remembered you
In the morning
With your head resting
Back, your eyes closed.

Lips together
Like there were no words
Left in the world.

I kissed you.

Looked out onto the street
And saw the snow in the trees,
A young boy in a blue cap
Riding his bike into the cold.

I turned back to you
But you had risen then;

And I watched you walk
Deeper into the house
Like a woman I never knew.

Your dress was wrinkled
And I thought about your hips.

We had already made love
And I wanted to kiss you again

So that you would believe
What I told you

About the wild horses
On the beach who eat
Out of stranger's hands

And come to me
In my dreams
Now, almost every night.

What Door Opens Like This

The nightmares I forget
And even the first time
We made love. It makes
Me shiver-sometimes I
Dream of icicles long
Slender and white. Spears
In the cave of my desire
The world will not let
Me sing us right. Dust
In the air. Sometimes
I watch the children play
And know they haven't
Learned righteousness yet.
I'll go back to sleep tonight
Wanting to dream something
Better. And I am not afraid.

What door opens like this?

Heaven #2

The cathedral where they baptized the child
Has ceilings high and bells and organs
And the soft sounds that make you drift
Down into the wooden pews and think

How great God is when you see the lonely
What do you say to them? Do you lie
About happiness or pull them towards
The great light? Do you speak of gospel?

Or do you say something silly and trivial?
I love you because you are a human being.
Do you look into their eyes to see
What they believe? If they are more than

Sinner? How do we know each blue note
And learn to sing the truth in it towards
Happiness? How do we say what's right
And not lie? Look me in the eye

And I'll tell you the many people
I have been. Some of them lonely
And others faces in a crowd walking
The city at night under the cathedral.

If you believe in more than what you see
Or the hollow sound of rain against the house
In the middle of summer, or that quiet
Filled with snow falling, you can also believe

In me and the imperfection of shotgun houses.
The poor town my father called home, the grave

Yard with weeds rising up over names, with dust
And mud and pine needles. Walk softly and listen.

What are you really trying to say, saying everything
Is not so bad, sometimes good. What do you mean?
Is it love or simply another rain falling in the wind?

for karla

the night with shoes
too small for your feet

the difference between
sorrow and disappointment

someone else's day
and the nights we make

love, the walk
through woods

while the wind
plays the trees

like a muted horn
trying to sing sorrow

we know it's more
than blues, we learn

to dance even
sad and lonely

our two-step
our back and forth

our feet walking
backwards, side

to side, going,

ONE SHOE MARCHING TOWARDS HEAVEN

in the same direction

your feet
so small

upon the earth
singing footsteps

rocking a child
in the middle
of the night
to sleep

onward

code: the koans begin

Some of the slaves grew depressed over their condition.
They got under before they got over.
Master's therapist who had studied
The great theories of the human spirit
Explained first that God would straighten things out;
But only if they worked hard at it. First God, God first
Then onto the philosophies of great men,
Many who believed a nigga was worthy of slavery.
He explained the ways one must approach a predicament with
The right frame of mind. "Whatever your do, don't run away.
You can't run away from your problems, you must stay
In the difficult position and deal with them. There
Is no freedom in running away."

Revisiting the Underground

1.

There is contraband here
In our hearts, the dictators
Are singing above the earth
With their spades cracking
Skulls and hallucinating
In the eternity of lies.

There is the stolen piece of bread
In our smiles, the joke dropped
Into the bottom of the sea that
Floats on down like a penny with
A wish on it.

There is the sorrow we cannot escape
Tattooed on our backs, an atom that
Weighs a ton on our tongues when
We talk back, stand up and fight
Stare them in the eye.

In the belly of the world someone
Is singing gospel, grinding seeds
In their palms, so that we
May have flour to make bread
Or dye to stain our souls with beautiful colors.

So when you see us marching again
Into the future like bright colored birds,
Don't stand between us and the truth.
For what you think is behind you
Is deep in our hearts right here right now.

2.

Not the heart made of secrets
Or the image, though it breathes
Out there in the abyss of cyberspace
In the static fuzz of T.V.

Not the mystery of your second coming
Or the splash of hips against your desire.
Not this week's new hype spinning
Out the windows of cars, or talking shit
On corners, not what is within you

That calls to what is without, not your mama
Or your cousins or fried fish sandwiches
At 2 A.M.,

Deeper than that.

Not being late or counting sheep or counting time
Or sitting outside talking about getting inside.
Not the fury that is hotter than July.
Not the fury that is dry as burnt toast.

Not the blackness you despise and love.
Not the dreams you visit smiling in a mirror.
Trying on new clothes, not your ancestors
You call X because there is no name.

That name and its belly,
That soup and its ingredients.
Yes, that thing, you carry
But cannot feel its weight.

3.

There will be wars and rumors of war.
Your mother will call you in from outside
From the heat and tell you to get something
To eat.

You will walk into the empty apartment
And microwave something late at night
And know hunger, feed the thing breeding
Inside you all day.

You have pickles in your mouth, olives,
Mustard in the refrigerator. You have red
Stains on your hands and barbeque chips.

You have shoe funk in your shoes, you have
Walked a long way. There will be songs
That were the shit that you will never hear again.
There will be fine ass women who turn into
Your grandmother. There will be fine ass men
Whose arms turn to Jell-O, there will be
Fights, anger, and despair that your children
Inherit as seeds.

There will be money that fades like jeans.
You will forget the stamps, what the price
Of postage was when you were a child.
You will forget the power of language.
You will tell stories and your heart will
Remain still, you will go down into Egypt
A million times.

4.

In the morning with dirt on your hands
You will plant flowers, you will play in the mud
Again, you will sing the lullaby to yourself
With no one to witness.

You will go to the concerts and watch
Your heroes die under the knife of history.
You will find in your closet shoes you
Never wore, shirts and skirts that stare
At you from the old days of time.

You'll chant the dust in your mouth.
What you've memorized about heaven
Will turn to mud, become earth again.

koan #7: the nationalist speaks of war

they whispered
war with their eyes. one
not yet won. one
we could not win. one
we had already lost. they
could not swim that far. you
can't swim that far. go.
they said go. where?
where you gonna go?

Song for The Country

The song of the country
Is in our hips, testament

Our celebrities celebrated
Names in the breeze. Say

Across the plains. Who shadowed
The shadow of the mountains?

It doesn't matter now. Men
Shapeshift the grief of their lives.

Someone's coming. I hear
The cloth on their back and wrists

Brush against the walls of the
Hallway. He's hungry in his

Sorrow. He's drunk with his words.
It's his freedom. He talks too much

And dreams out loud.
He wants to debate
Everything.

It's his democracy.
That troubles him so.

Solo on Rage

Race is a dry patch of land where nothing grows
Without water, shriveled and wrinkled, living
But looking like death, bottom poor yield, the tiny fruit
Almost still born, almost dead. There is land like this
All over America, some rented to the sons
And daughters of those who worshipped heaven
As a place where white folks lived and did the Lord's
Work, the more ambitious buy a piece of it knowing
It's better than nothing, the lazy and shiftless spit
In the dust, curse the mule and wander behind it
Working that same land for nothing for nothing.
When you think of the thief and the gambler, the
Bandanna wearing bravado of youth with rage,
Remember the land that does not give, the ankle
Bracelet for crimes, leniency, and secret profit,
Years of hard work for pennies, of the man enslaved
By crimes he did not commit, the burned down
And blown up churches, and the one story I
Would like to tell you in the parlor so that you can
Try to prove with words what has already
Happened, with your litmus test for sorrow, your
Research and craft, to have me rise above land
Damn near worthless, to have me become something
That might profit you. You will be famous and someone
Will finally believe the song that floats my words
Towards healing. I will say thank you, and you
Will go off excited that you can make money
And right the wrong in the world. I know better
Because the sun has baked my brain, the funerals
Seem to sink the sun, the rain that day said
Healing and horror and we wondered flood or nurture.
If I told you the truth you would call me bitter.

It would be so ugly you could not tell it again.
I treat you like I treat them, whoever the hell they
Are, they require story because what's not said
Helps them nurture their lies. As story worships
Its listener, the dictator doesn't want to listen,
Will kill you for that shit, what can you do?
Hasn't it always been this way, shoe shine boy,
Fiddler, and sandman, got your gutbucket blues
With moonshine, and the world closes in differently
On those who worked hard all week, nothing
But a street corner in one of your God forsaken cities,
Where everything cost where I sing for free.
They would like us to skip rage, though
The country is littered with mistakes and bones,
The deeds of men and women who are
Fallible. As though success comes from
Perfection, the myth of the white cloth, cotton,
Goddamn boll weevil in the sky who eats
The clouds, who eats the rain. I'm headed home
Now, no more stories to tell, truth is I'd rather
Yell and you have no idea what the fuck I'm
Saying, know what I'm saying, I'm just saying.

ONE SHOE MARCHING TOWARDS HEAVEN

when massa speak of freedom

you best not bring a book
or look words up in the dictionary.

matter fact, don't trust any word
unless it come out his mouth.

and you standing there in sunshine
watching the smile on his face.

you gotta know what day it is
what season erupts underneath
the constitution of ideas;

otherwise, call it music, dance
to it follow it with your eyes;

but don't let your heart get caught
up in that conversation:

> *old folks who believe in heaven*
> *but ain't never been there*

if there's anything on paper
make a copy of it and put it
in the old bible, in a firebox

and hope to god
you don't never have to use it.

my dream starring the devil

the river ran backwards and the music in the world
sounded like heavy metal and murder, my daddy
came up from his grave and asked what the fuck
is you doing son? and he don't curse. i drove out
one morning with bacon on my breath to find
all the stop signs had disappeared. new orleans
men who skipped the dirge now singing hallelujah.
everything changed, but I didn't trust em. they say
you gotta go down into the basement and find
you some a them ole boots that ain't ever gonna
shine no more, cuz where we going there's plenty
a mud. they lead me past the church and my grandma's
singing the sanest prayers to white jesus mixed
with blood, fear, and things she ain't never
told nobody. down on to the river where it waits
for me like a woman whose husband been out
all night long. right where it bends, and cuts into
the earth. it toss and turn muddy water mist
in the air. that's when angels start sharpening
their blades, water rises, and tiny drops glint
in the sunlight. they say jump in, and sweet song
jesus like he coming back; but fear shook me
like a shopkeeper who caught me putting little
candies into my pocket, somewhere my mother
cried out asking where's my boy? i couldn't do it.
what had I become? i went barefoot back
into the woods with a lust stretched over my head
like a stocking cap, the line on my forehead running
east to west. the woods filled with men who drank
blood calling nigger dangerous jokes, aberrations
eating flesh stoking fire, rubbing their bellies

ONE SHOE MARCHING TOWARDS HEAVEN

chanting freedom like a pagan idol, freedom
pickling hate stomping babies to death
tattooing brains with nightmares, worshipping
fear as a god and offering sacrifice. they killed
me and said this is your inheritance. home
i asked and sought, tapped out on the earth
beneath me, home like morse code
in a dark sea. without the thirst of the long traveler
you might say it's funny, but i always ate
and drank kool-aid laced with sugar, ham hocks,
the eggs and pork brains, the scrapple, little
colored bubblegum, taste as forgetting, some
cane sweet syrup, some molasses, some dying
home where lying could not lie. whisper they said
the bible says, get on your knees, pray, show
some respect for the cadillac and elegance
can't, we won't, stop on a dime, bring it back
up, sip iced tea with just a little bit of whiskey;
but it ain't all that bad. there's that big bright moon
that keep coming no matter how bad things look
and when she shine something in me still sing
there's everything to get over, but nothing like
morning. i watch it all the time, creep into
the houses and make people rise, walk, and cook.
birds sing and shit, squirrels stop stutter and look
at me, the bees, and the flies, until the dusk sinks
heavy at the doorstep of those who dance heavy
with breath. a cool glass of water my friend.
something simple. the long hard day men sang
about, the dying sun who goes home every night
cuz shit don't stay hot forever. concrete pillars glow
in the dark painted neon showing you the way
to kill yourself, the old men said that's the point.
then you'll forget how to dream bones, no more
silk dresses with lace trim for your wife, you won't

be able to make it happen ever again. what matters
now: it's almost fall and there's a dying in the earth
every human being knows, like the earth is hungry
and one knows the coming is fear and agony.
the devil came to me and told me this. this
is your story he say. i was stupid enough to listen.

ONE SHOE MARCHING TOWARDS HEAVEN

Elijah Muhammad

jacob wrestled with the angel
birthrights had been at stake

night a drape of black silk
white light spilling onto everything

the parables were broken stories
mumbled in the mouths of men

was been christians who led
themselves to water then found

god in tiny storefront churches
with the crescent and moon

overhead, fascinating, impossible
some of them were genius

their bow ties shiny and perfect,
and others were money, mission-

aries without understanding,
jungle and gunshot, nighttime

hot spots, newspapers and bean
pies, and the devil, always amongst

us, with insurance, and prices too
high, a shotgun behind the counter

an angry machine, a bulldozer,
a fiery furnace, a war machine

a dream of manifest destiny,
jacob wrestled with the angel

he sung spirituals until his voice
was hoarse, something died in him

something was born, his thigh
shriveled but his back straightened up

who is the devil?
what is hate?

everafter

koan # 57: the blowing wind

can you imagine
them imagining
there was something
they couldn't imagine
that you had imagined

Home

I think of home and
I think of all the rain
In this city, all the rain
In the world, in the world.

All the music, all the people
All the dancing, all the love.
As I prepare to come home
I think of all the music.

The drum in the city
The burning of the city
The city going down
The city rising up

Love and flesh, the cold
In the summer, the blood,
The trees making beauty
With grace and forever.

I forget my name.
I forget the names
I have been called.
Many things I have been,

Some of them like you
Some of them cold and lonely
Some of them dust
Some of them rising up.

The thousand feet
The sound of rain

The bird's song
The going down

The rising up,
Lonely as a steeple
Pointing to forever.
They'll call me crazy.

Yes, they love me.
Yes, they always will.

Now the sun rises.
Yes, I'll come home
With less and more
With heaven and hell

With the clothes I wear
With the birds
With the singing
With the drum

Tuned to a different pitch.
Hungry and full
Lonely and gathered together
In the name of.

the gods

what do you know of the gods,
young man, as you scrape
against the earth with the blade
of your hunger, worshipping
what becomes, what is seen?

to cut the drummer's hands
or murder the priest, say devil
like you mean it, swim back
to africa, spit in the face
of holiness. say death

to the gods and mean it:
jus' business, capitalism,
the merry go round horses
that go up and down, sticks
of beauty, impossible beauty.

if you creep into the city
where I was born at night
men chant to dice, and sing
over the tiny reed of a bottle:
what could never be clean

cut and butchered like certain.
they know, but won't know
unless it's a secret. i go down
like smoke into lungs, like
sorrow in the dirge after death.

that seductive music makes
men feel alive, it calls us out
the house like a gunshot

thunderclap white light
twisting through clouds:

*come to me, know my magic
shake and shiver, get down.*

ONE SHOE MARCHING TOWARDS HEAVEN

on reading Jack Gilbert too late at night

the t.v. talks,
but i don't listen;
and outside the warm fall day
fades away under a thin slivered moon.

there's no silence in the house
but two empty glasses of wine,
two dark black guinness bottles
mouths without words towards morning.

"don't leave me now", she says
with her eyes, a woman i knew
once in a city of asphalt, a moan
goes up into the night, wisp

of smoke. i go outside to take
a cigarette, and the moon stares
at me; but its eye is squinted
the cool air coming in.

free black space

if there is dust on the furniture
in my mother's house, the symbol
is the lampshade. when the sun
goes down, we turn the lights on,
people speak that ole talk,
somebody catches themself
falling up the stairs, somebody
whispers white man, dust as cloud,
what the silent speak when there
are no voices around to tell them
telling is wrong, to tell them sick,
is a country, to tell them freedom,
justice, democracy, a tiny circle
where we sing heaven and breathe
hard into a cloud of smoke, this
is my rhyme, my heavy heart, my
shit spoke, so dope, youngns choked
like it was reefer smoke, my momma
plays word games, my grandma plays
word games, my granddaddy casts
himself as silent in the face of men
with pistols. i like the boy screaming
out what the fuck is going on in here,
way his pants sag, now i can name
disrespect, now i can say my name,
say my name, like sex, stocking caps,
a rim around the hairline, make waves,
come correct, my sister crying under
a comb, crying for my daddy to come
home, we never say that, all us gathered.

we were chasing a microphone, we

wanted the true sermon of the street
corner to become gospel, we wanted
to worship with the men who walked
in ways we couldn't, those who saved
and spent it on a cadillac of cool
lean back high and hard bass lines,
cabarets, and pulled pork, too much
hot sauce, a good christmas, when
we stood in those lines, we still
appeared to be in a circle, we were
waiting for the voice of god, the voice
of the ancestors, for people
who looked like us to say something
that would say what's in words
floats on the sea of this world;
but the sea is in me, the sea is in us.

koan #58: late joy

all night we talked.
talked shit, the shit
we been through
like it was just talk.

we ate too,
like it was just eating.

we drank wine
and sometimes
we sang the wine in us.

when we ain't have much
we talked more,
or just silent with each other,

usually after the sun
had gone down.
we came up like that.

talking too much
even talking the talk talked about,
that we talk too much.

owning the joy
of the night is not too hard.
yeah i know it's hard;

but sometimes,
when we talk that talk
it really ain't.

ONE SHOE MARCHING TOWARDS HEAVEN

for baraka

afraid i did not understand
afraid to say, mom, the weather
outside is cold, too cold for you
to go out, today another happening
like yesterday, that happened;
unfortunately, the magic dull as
the weather, hot as the sun, look
into the sky, no future, i see no future,
because i know what things mean,
the suited men are an army, the letters
are contracts coming before war,
the heat is a metaphor for pressure,
a hand in a fitted leather glove, against
itself. when i say, that's my man, that
shit was dope, when i say   damn!
and my breath is part of a storm, does
that sign my ignorance, my legacy of
hate, the ignorant heart of the uneducated?
i choose simple shit to lose my temper
to, sing the song my ancestors could
not sing, to not say what you mean,
thought as air, rising and pressed down
compacted thought, hip hop when it was
a seed, jazz when it was forever looking
back the way we came. that baraka,
strong nigger feeling. i feel that shit.
everyday. everyday. i funk with it. sway.

koan #64: not yet forever

the best thought
is the thought
about thinking
and knowing
thought's importance

i used to think that

how important
i thought
it was

ONE SHOE MARCHING TOWARDS HEAVEN

The Miner Speaks of the Underground

I mined
I minded
I minded the mines
I minded the mines forever
Mining forever is hope
The tired religion
The tried and tired religion
I tried and tried to sing on top
But I am a miner

Who loves the underground
Under the ground I hold and hollow
Out the earth, under the earth I know
My business underground, always been
Underground, my business the mines
I minded

Each morning I sink into the earth
Birds singing as I go down the song
As I go down, the song of going down
The song going down into the black earth
The song of death. The song of work
Underneath the earth, smoke, cough,
Taking breath under the earth is bad
Breath, we breathe the breath of long singers
Under the earth, we take a pickaxe and machine
To stone and pitch weight, mud, moist, rock
We rock and swing, sing and swing deep under
The earth, do the dance that is a hard day's work
We sing:

    Day do what day do

Day overhead
Day do what do is doing
Day overhead

Sing and swing sing and swing
Somebody bring me my hammer
God knows, only God knows
Somebody bring me my hammer

There's no steel like will
There's nothing to steal under
The earth there's nothing to steal, even,
Steady now, that's the song we sing, say
We crazy for going down, there in the morning
It still looks like night. There in the morning
The stillness looks like night.

They say this underground like dying
But damn they love my song, they say
Damn that man can sing, but they hate
This underground, they think they know,
Oh Lord they think they know, they think
They know this underground sound

They don't know no Ogun, they don't know
No hammer, but Lord they love this song,
They sing and they sing it, but don't wanna be
Don't wanna be like me, don't wanna be underground
Don't wanna sing no underground, don't wanna be
In the dark, don't wanna be underground, don't
Wanna be in the night, and that's alright, that's why
I mine, and mind my own business, in the underground

That's why I sing the tired and tried religion
That's why I mined the mines

ONE SHOE MARCHING TOWARDS HEAVEN

That's why I mind my own business
That's why I sing the way I do.